The Road to My Old
KENTUCKY HOME

Vickie Curtsinger

Copyright © 2018 by Vickie Curtsinger

The Road to My Old **KENTUCKY HOME**

All rights reserved. No part of this publication may be reproduced, distributed, or transmitted in any form or by any means, including photocopying, recording, or other electronic or mechanical methods, without the prior written permission of the publisher, except in the case of brief quotations embodied in critical reviews and certain other noncommercial uses permitted by copyright law. For permission requests, write to the publisher, addressed "Attention: Permissions Coordinator," at info@beyondpublishing.net

Quantity sales special discounts are available on quantity purchases by corporations, associations, and others. For details, contact the publisher at the address above.

Orders by U.S. trade bookstores and wholesalers. Email info@BeyondPublishing.net

The Beyond Publishing Speakers Bureau can bring authors to your live event. For more information or to book an event contact the Beyond Publishing Speakers Bureau speak@BeyondPublishing.net

The Author can be reached directly https://beyondpublishing.net/AuthorVickieCurtsinger

Manufactured and printed in the United States of America distributed globally by BeyondPublishing.net

New York | Los Angeles | London | Sydney

10 9 8 7 6 5 4 3 2 1   978-1-947256-30-9

Hardcover May 2018

"The Road to My Old Kentucky Home has a way of taking you back in time for a moment....it's like a crash course on "the good ole days!" A must-read especially for locals."

Amy Raney

My dad was born in 1940, on October 8th, in Laurel County, Kentucky. My mother was born in 1942, on May 3rd, in Knox County, Kentucky. They didn't live more than about eight to ten miles apart. They met and started dating in 1959. In those days, they asked you to be their girlfriend, and the men usually asked the girls for dates. My dad came from a large family of eleven kids, and my mother came from a family of seven kids. They were married in June of 1960, with only their parents and the minister that wed them.

We worked at a gas station in London, Kentucky, and, in those days, they pumped the gas for the customers. My father told me when he started driving, you didn't have to have a driver's license, nor did you have to have insurance on your car. After having a couple of kids, they moved to Richmond, Kentucky, and they added a few more children to their growing family. They moved again, from Rose Hill, Kentucky to Tatham, Kentucky, and that's when I came along.

Mom and dad moved to Tatham, (Willisburg) Kentucky in 1974, where my father had bought a farm. They had five children: two boys and three girls. They had lived in Tatham for about a year before I came into the picture on a cold December day in 1975.

My mom had five children at the hospital, and my sister Brenda came in the car! With me, she decided she wasn't going to the hospital. She had already told my dad, so he knew she meant it, and it scared him to death! In those days they didn't let the father go in with the mother when they were in labor or about to give birth, and with a home birth, he would not only be present for the first time, he would be the one delivering me.

Around eleven a.m., my mom told my oldest brother, Wesley, to take my youngest brother, Tony, to the barn, because she said she was getting ready to have me! My other siblings, the three girls— Connie, age 13, Brenda, age 12, and Linda, age 9— were at Mt. Olivet Baptist Church. The preacher, Bro. Lowell Cantrell, had picked them up and taken them there earlier. Wesley went to tell my dad, who was taking a nap on the couch.

All the times Dad had thought of the prospect of delivering me, it scared him to death, but, for some reason, when it was upon him, he was calm as a cucumber! He put on the kettle of water to boil. Then, he boiled a string to tie around my umbilical cord and sterilized the scissors with alcohol. I was face-down when my mom gave birth to me, and my dad said he had considered turning me over before I was all the way out, but thought, "Better not!" He helped pull me out, turned me over, and spanked me to get me to cry.

Mom urged him, "Hand her to me!" Apparently, she fooled with me until she got me to crying.

An hour later, dad went to pick up the girls from church, about two miles down the road in Tatham. When the girls got in the truck he told them, "Well, you got a baby sister at home." They tell me he was excited, relieved, and nervous all at once.

When they got back, mom told dad she wanted to take me to the hospital, so they could check me out. Mom told the nurses at James B. Haggin Memorial Hospital, in Harrodsburg, Kentucky she had delivered me at home. They told her that made their day!

I was born in "the white house", as they called it, on Tatham Road, in Willisburg, Kentucky. From time to time, my mom would take us children to Henry Royalty's, an old general store in the community of Tatham Springs. I've come to love little general stores so much, because, now, they remind me of a bygone era as they close, replaced by big box stores.

That was where the "big 4-H camp" was, or at least that's what they called it when I was young. It was right behind Henry Royalty's store and across an old rusty, iron bridge over Tatham River. I must say, I never liked that bridge! It always gave me the creeps driving over it!

Just after the bridge was Mt. Olivet Baptist Church, where my mother would go and play her guitar and sing from time to time. It was a lovely little community with so much history! I'll never forget the memories and history of ghost towns like the one I grew up in, communities where people would come from miles upon miles, just to hang out.

The old 4-H camp was a huge building that always mesmerized me! It was actually a hotel called Tatham Springs Hotel and Spa on Carey Island. It was built on the Chaplin River in the late 1800s and had a sulfur spring on the back portion of the land. The Hotel had fifty-three rooms, a spa, nine acres, and it even had an in-ground swimming pool. The two-story building was shaped in the letter E and had a variety of recreational options, including: tennis courts, bowling, masquerade balls, and billiards. For our time, it was a very modern resort.

An ad that appeared in the *Kentucky Gazette* in 1896, described Tatham Springs as a health resort in Washington County with a social season that usually lasted the hot months of June, July, and August. Boarding rates were fifteen dollars per week. In its prime, the hotel hosted famous people like Franklin D. Roosevelt and General Patton. He bathed, drank, swam, and canoed in its waters. Tatham Springs Hotel and Spa catered to affluent Kentuckians who flocked there to bath in and drink the mineral waters that could help them escape the yellow fever and malaria. The spas of the time boasted mineral water that was guaranteed to promote health. Other well-known 19th century spas included: Graham Springs in Harrodsburg, Crab Orchard Springs in Lincoln County, Blue Licks Spring in Nicholas County, and Cerulean Springs in Trigg County. These all became the most fashionable spas in Kentucky.

With the invention of the automobile and the Great Depression, most of the Kentucky spas closed by the 1920s, including Tatham Springs Hotel and Spa. Sadly, on May of 2006, it burnt to the ground, the history gone but not forgotten by all who had seen it or experienced its glory days.

Another place we visited as children was Henry Royalty's General Merchandise Store. My mom and dad took us there to purchase the necessities. Henry Royalty owned the store from 1953 through 1990. Over the years, he changed the name from Henry Royalty's General Merchandise to Royalty's Grocery. It burned in a fire sometime around 2010.

In 1978, we moved to the little community of Mayo, in the city of Harrodsburg, Kentucky. I was only three years old. The name of our road, Indian Creek, always intrigued me as a child. I always thought it must have been Indians who lived back on that dead-end mile of a road. I would always beg my sister Brenda to take me to Mayo Store to get me a soda, and she would usually give in. There were two stores in Mayo. They were just across the street from each other.

As a child, I went to both stores. I didn't realize how much history these stores held, precious memories of people long gone. One year, around the time I was eleven years old, my parents bought me a moped. I rode that moped up to the B&S Store, where my dad had a tab we could charge things to, to get gas and soda. Farmers would sit on the old front porch talking and watching the cars go by.

I never imagined that, one day, these thriving stores would no longer exist. In 1885, John T. Voris had a store in almost the same spot, and there is still a store there today. The store was the center of activity in the community as we knew it. Van B. Carter owned it from 1900 until A.R. Brown purchased it from him in 1920.

In those days, families came from miles around to buy and sell at the store. You could find anything you wanted, and, if you couldn't, A.R. Brown would get it for you. He would buy and sell eggs. My dad said people came from all over, even in the late 70s.

Wendell Johnson said he worked for A.R. Brown, and, for several years, he drove a truck to deliver all over. Whatever he could make money at, he sold. He said there was no quitting time. It was a lot of hard work! "I guess you could call them the good ole days," said his wife. He and his wife went to Fairview School down the road, about three or four miles from A.R. Brown's store in Mayo. A.R. Brown owned and ran the store for roughly sixty years. In 1980, Jim Burns and Wallace Shepperson bought the store, and Shepperson owned it until he passed away, in 2010. The Minks bought it, and it has sat vacant ever since.

I lived in Mayo most of my life. I married in October of 1994 and had two daughters. In 2001, we built a home on Indian Creek Road. We sold it in 2008, and moved to the town we bought land in, on Long Lane. We built again and sold again. We were gone a total of seven years. In 2015, we purchased the old Meaux property on Indian Creek, in Mayo. We were back home now! No matter where I lived, Mayo and Indian Creek Road was always home to me.

My parents and brother own property on Indian Creek Road, as well. Like the old saying goes, "There's no place like home." Mayo has just always been home, no matter how long I was gone. I never loved another place like I love Mayo.

One day, I decided I wanted to photograph all the old general stores and the little community I had grew up in, so I ventured out to my birthplace's community and store, only to be shocked to find out they were no longer standing! Henry Royalty's old store was gone. The 4-H Camp, Tatham Springs and Spa, Mt. Olivet Baptist Church—all gone. Even the creepy old iron bridge was gone!

The memories I held onto in my mind was all that was left. I was so sad! I had heard that the store and the old 4-H/Spa had burned down, but I didn't expect it all to be gone. I started my journey on a quest to research and find the history behind these old stores and homesteads and to photograph the remaining stores in Mayo and surrounding communities that were still standing, but are no longer in business; abandoned.

In June of 2017, I ventured out to take pictures of B&S Store in Mayo, the Don/Grey's store in Mayo, and other stores all around. All have closed or no longer cease to exist, having been torn or burnt down. I find it so sad that a part of our history, what we dubbed as "the good ole days," the days when folks would gather to play cards or checkers, eat a bologna sandwich with coke and peanuts, talking of the day's work and chores and lots of laughing—now gone.

Old country general stores just no longer exist. But B&S store is still standing. I told my husband, if I had my dreams, I would own a boutique, or own the old B&S Store, or own a bed and breakfast.

As of November of 2017, I own the old B&S Store in Mayo. The same store I had visited as a child, until it closed its doors. It never crossed my mind that these old stores would be gone, no longer running as I once remembered them. Or that I'd be operating the same country, history-filled general store that had such a significance in the little community of Mayo, for over one hundred years!

To me, this store is beautiful! In its glory days, it was one of the nicer stores of the time. The architecture is so nice for a little old general store. It has a beautiful skylight in the twelve-foot ceilings of wood. It boasts wooden floors, wooden bookshelf cases, and even an old wooden plank porch, as well as a tin roof and tin siding. I'm thrilled to have the opportunity to put Mayo back on the map with this one-hundred-year-old, original general store.

When I was five years old, I would go to church in Washington County with my mom. We lived in Mayo, but still had strong ties to Willisburg. There was a small church that sat on a hill. Inside, it was not very big at all; maybe eight hundred square feet, but everyone knew each other. The small church was mostly made up of family. At the age of eight, I started to go to another church with my older siblings, Connie and Linda. That church was between Willsburg and Springfield, Kentucky. The church was called Hillsboro, and I had a lot of friends who attended services there. It sat way back on a dead-end road, made up mostly of curves and Hillsboro and country homes. To a small child, the church seemed so old. It was much older than the other church I had previously attended with my mom. I recall many nights in the late 70s when we would swing by Hume's grocery on our way home, to get snacks and sodas. Our choices included Funyuns potato chips, Vienna sausages, and, of course, Pepsi.

Another country store, about two miles from Robert Hume's store, was Carriers Grocery. We would stop in when I was only two, again, for snacks and drinks. It was bigger and built different than the Hume's store. It was kind of an odd shape for a general store.

On March 28, 1935, *The Springfield* Sun stated that a curio, discovered by a Willisburg man several days earlier, estimated to be more than 150 years old, was a fine specimen. He had found an Indian peace pipe on his farm near Willisburg, close to Hillsboro Church. Even though it had been in the ground for over a century, it was in great condition. The old pipe measured ten inches long and four inches in circumference. At one end was a neatly carved squirrel's head. The stone from which the pipe had been carved is not found in this part of the country. It is almost certain that it was once the property of an Indian chief.

In early times, the Indians came to this area for their annual hunts. Their favorite grounds for camping during the hunting season was near the Hillsboro Church. The pipe was found one mile from the church. Many other curios of Indian days have been found in the same area. There are such neat parts of history in all our backyards!

I remember one Easter Sunday, in 1983, I went to church as usual, with my older sister, Connie. She was the oldest of the four girls. At the time, she was around twenty-one years old, and I was only eight. The pastor of Hillsboro Church was Cathy Cheatham. After she delivered the message, I wanted to go up to the altar and pray. She came and prayed with me, and I gave my heart to the Lord that Easter Sunday!

Even though I was young, I was so excited to go to church. It seemed as if I didn't want the service to end that night. I couldn't wait for the next church service! I was eager to tell everyone what had happened in my life and the decision I had just made. A year after I got saved, I was baptized in the Tatham River, under that rusty old bridge.

Hillsboro Church holds a very special place in my heart. As a young girl, I would have so much fun with my friends after church, playing dodgeball in the field to the right of the church. I'll never forget them letting me teach the smaller children in Sunday school. It was a small church, and, since it was a one-room building, the walls of our "classrooms" were merely curtains that slid and partitioned off rooms. You could hear the other teachers talking, but it never seemed too loud.

It had no running water and only had an outhouse. In the early 80s, a lot of churches still used outhouses. To the left of the church was an old graveyard. We had church there until mid-to-late 80s, and built a church right next to Highway 55. The new church had running water, many rooms, two bathrooms, and a basement with additional rooms. I would later go to church with my mom and dad in Harrodsburg, Kentucky, to the Harrodsburg Church of God.

I have known my husband since I was a young girl—I was five, and he was twelve, so I don't remember much about him. We both attended the same church in Willisburg. He says he remembers me, sitting in the back with my friend, Karen, who was four years older than me. My husband says I'd be chewing my bubble gum and writing on a notebook or looking at picture albums.

Later—sometime around 1992—he would begin working for my dad,. My dad was a carpenter and had a construction business. I recall seeing him come to our house sometimes, to ride to work with my dad. His cousin worked for my dad, too. My dad was a builder of homes, pole barns, roofing—just about anything one could build, he did.

Later, Johnnie—my husband—moved into a trailer next door and rented it from my dad, along with his cousin, Tim. They both had previously lived in Washington County while we lived on Indian Creek in Mayo. I remember walking up past the trailer, because we had a basketball goal up the road that my older brothers and dad had put up years earlier. It joined the road and had a little pad poured next to the blacktop road. Many times, I never knew if Johnnie or Tim were home. Later, I found out they were home more than I ever knew.

One day, I left a note for Johnnie, inviting him and Tim to come to my older sister's house, in Chaplin, which was right next door to his previous hometown. It said we were going to have a bonfire and cookout, and they were invited to come. Well, he never came! Later, I saw him at The Bloomfield Tobacco Festival, in Bloomfield, Kentucky. My sister and I, along with his cousin, Debbie, were all walking around the festival when I heard someone holler at me. I turned around swiftly to see who it was, and it turned out to be Johnnie and his brothers. He said, "Hey! You wanna go to a dance?" They were having one later, nearby. I replied that I better not, because I thought he had another girlfriend, so I didn't want to get mixed up in all that.

About a month or so later, Johnnie and his cousin were cleaning out our landscaping. We talked some that day. It wasn't long until I ran into his dad at the E Z Stop store in Washington County, when I stopped by to get some lunch after stripping tobacco. His dad was an outgoing man.

He said, "Hey, my son has been planning on asking you out!"

I said, "He is?"

He replied, "He's not said anything to you?"

I said, "No."

He laughed and said, "Well, he will be." That took me by surprise.

 A couple of weeks before that, a few of us ladies had a lady's day out in Lexington. My friend, Karen, and I were sitting in the back of a small church van when, all of a sudden, our whole seat just flipped backwards after they took off from a red light! All you could see from up front were our feet! They were all just laughing hysterically at us, while we were trying to get up. They never did let us forget about that happening.

Later that day, Johnnie's cousin, who was with us, told me, "He's going to ask you out. He likes you."

I replied, "Really? His dad told me the same thing!"

She said, "Well, he's planning on it."

Later, his cousin that worked for my dad told me that he was wanting to ask me out, too. I told him "Well, his dad and cousin have told me. Now, you. How come he hasn't already?"

He answered, "I don't know, but he will."

Finally, in December of 1993, he asked me out! We got married in October of 1994. A few months later, I was pregnant with our first child. She was born November 9, 1995. Later, we had another child, a second daughter, born on October 12, 1998. I always wanted a boy and thought about trying again, but soon talked myself out of that!

In 2003, I started teaching the teens class at Harrodsburg Church of God, where I had been attending services since I was twelve. At the age of twenty-eight, I was having a lot of fun with my group of teenagers. A couple of them were my nephews. Teaching the class made me feel like I really had a purpose in life. It helped me to grow and learn a lot about the Bible, myself, because I had to study the Word. Whereas, before, I just read it to myself. I had always been so shy that stepping out of my comfort zone to teach the class helped me a whole lot.

I'd plan fun days outside of church, and we would take little field trips. One of them was to Mammoth Cave, Kentucky. Another was to Lexington, to the mall and movie, and another to Kentucky Kingdom. We had cookouts at Perryville Battlefield, in Perryville, Kentucky, and on Sunday, after church, I'd let them come home with us to ride four-wheelers and swim. We even had lock-ins at the church, where we'd have them arrive at 7 p.m. and leave at 7 a.m.! We had lots and lots of good fun and good times. Many memories were made.

I had parents who would come and tell me I had done such a good job with their kids and that they could really see such a difference in them! That really made my day back then, because that is what it was all about. Impacting their lives enough that they could see or feel a real difference.

In the meantime, I had become the church choir leader at our church. It grew well, considering the size church we had! It was fun to work with the group I had, even though I had never led a choir before! I was over that for about two to three years.

When I was about twelve, I decided to learn how to play the piano, because I had always wanted to play in church. We had an old antique piano in our house. I went to the Christian bookstore one day and noticed a piano book that showed the white keys. I memorized them on my way home, where I marked the white keys on the piano and taught myself to play a few notes. Later, I learned to key a song, but it usually took me an hour or longer to do. I put it on the back burner for a few years, just playing around every now and again, but never really getting too serious about it.

One year after I was married, my husband bought me a keyboard for Christmas! My mother had always been musically inclined, and she could play just about any instrument she picked up. She could even play Johnny Cash's songs as well as he could—or better, I thought! I asked her to see if I could

The Road to My Old Kentucky Home | 15

follow her on some church songs. I took my keyboard to her house, and she got out her guitar. She played, and I knew I could play just a little by ear. I tried to follow her, and, to my surprise, I did better than I imagined I would!

I kept practicing and practicing, and it wasn't long before I was playing in our church. For several years, I played as the main pianist at the church, in the place of the pastor's wife, who had gotten sick with cancer. I still play to this day. It was just something I had always wanted to do, so I did it!

If you ever want to do something, just try! Believe in yourself, and don't give up when you get frustrated. Keep on! Before you know it, you will be doing what you've always wanted to do!

It didn't come to me as soon as I wanted it, but after working and working for several years later, it came to me. By believing in myself, not giving up on my dream of playing the piano, and practicing, I was able to achieve my goal. Like they say, practice makes perfect!

Nine times out of ten, your dreams are within reach! It's in your sights—just persevere! I truly believe if you can dream it, you can do it! Take one step at a time, and, before you know it, you can be on your way to starting your own business or whatever dream you set out to achieve! Do your research on how you want to get started, everything you need to know, and what to do. No one in their right mind would try to fly a plane without the proper training needed for the job! Just like you wouldn't want to jump in to starting or owning a business without doing your research and developing a plan first. Make the plan, try to map out how you are going to operate it and how to work it.

Plan your finances. sit down and count the cost. Luke 14:28-30, in the King James Bible, tells us:

> *For which of you, intending to build a tower, sitteth not down first, and counteth the cost, whether he have sufficient to finish*

it? Lest haply, after he hath laid the foundation, and it not able to finish it, all that behold it begin to mock him, Saying, this man began to build, and was not able to finish.

In other words, it's not wise to not count the cost or sit down with a pen and paper and figure out the cost of everything first!

There are a few questions you should ask yourself. Is there a need for your business, products, or services? Do you have a plan? If so, write it down. What are the costs? A small business may not require a lot of money, but it will cost you some to invest in your products. My banker requires a projection of what I think all my costs will total for the year, as well as a projection of what I will make for the year. Even though there is no way to be 100 percent certain, I sit down and think about what it will cost and what I might profit. I write down a list of all costs, including: electric, payroll, stock, and my own pay. If you don't have the funds to start your business, there may be grants and small business loans you qualify for.

Choose your businesses name. It will play an important role in the business, so you want it to be a good one. Choose one you won't want to change later. Get all the licenses and permits you need to start. You'll need to research which ones you will need for the type of business you are starting.

Consider your businesses location. Does it serve its purpose where it is located? For instance, locating a store that only sold bedding or clothing in the country is unlikely to serve its purpose where it is located, because there is not a great need for such a store in the country. On the other hand, a store selling food, ice, or drinks would serve its purpose well. It would fulfill a need.

If you are considering having employees, plan out how many, and plan the duties of each job before you begin your business. You will also need a tax preparer who you can use to take care of your business, or you can choose to do it yourself.

Also, promote your business! You need to start getting customers and advertising. Utilizing social media is a great way to get people to learn about you and your business. Plan, write, and act on the steps. Just remember: if your business doesn't take off flying, don't just give up! Keep doing the best you can do and work hard. Eventually, hard work pays off.

Steps to starting
A BUSINESS

Step 1: Believe in yourself and have faith! Be positive!

Step 2: Get mentally prepared. Begin by becoming business-minded. Read books on success and books about business.

Step 3: Go for it! Step outside of your comfort zone. Don't be afraid to take chances. If you're never willing to take a chance, how do you know if you can or can't? If you fall, get back up again! You may have to go into debt to start your business, but if you're not rich, it is often the only way to start a large business.

I had to take my husband outside of his comfort zone to start a business. After much persuading, I finally talked him into it. I said, "Let's just try it out! How are we going know if we don't try?" So, that year he went into business for himself doing gutters and construction. He did really well! You must believe it will do well and work hard at it! Don't give up if it slows down. Just keep working at it!

Step 4: Don't be afraid to advertise! Social media is one great tool for advertising, but there are other ways, too — newspapers, custom made t-shirts with your business name on them, yard signs, business cards, etc. Pass out business cards to everyone you know, and tell them what your business is about! Believe in yourself and be confident. Do your job as though you were doing it for yourself. Treat clients as you would want someone to treat you, and there's almost no room to fail. Treat them well, and they will advertise for you! Word of mouth is the best advertisement you can get, and it comes by treating your clients/customers right and by doing an excellent job!

Along my journey of starting my own business in 2008, the owner of one of the stores in our community of Mayo (whom I had known all my life growing up, from visiting his store as a young child, up until the present, when I was bringing in my own children) was getting up there in age. He had run the store for many years and was now ready to retire. He asked me and my husband to take over.

At that time, I had never really considered becoming a store owner. As I began to ponder on it, I would lay awake at night, thinking of all that I would like to do with the little country store. I thought of the food I would like to carry and how I would run things, and I would get so excited I couldn't sleep! But, then, I'd start to think, "I can't do this! I've never run a country store before!" I eventually allowed the negative thoughts to outweigh the positive until I had talked myself right out of it.

During that time, we lived only 500 yards from both stores in Mayo. Our property on Central Pike Road joined up to the Mayo Christian Church and, then, joined B&S Grocery. Later, I learned that this property all belonged to Van B. Carter, the former owner of B&S in 1900. He then sold it to A.R. Brown, who became the owner after him. It was a several-hundred-acre farm that had been divided. My land was once a part of the B&S Store farm.

A few years later, we moved from there to Long Lane, in Harrodsburg. We built a home there. I must say, we had one the most beautiful views in Mercer County! We could see for miles away. The house sat upon a hill that overlooked the vast countryside. We were told it was one of the highest—if not the highest—point in Mercer County. In the summer, we could see several 4th of July fireworks displays, from Anderson Dean Park's display in Mercer County, to Garrard County, and several others, far off in the distance. We decided to sell the mini farm.

From the time I was just a little girl, I had wanted to purchase this land that had sat vacant on Indian Creek Road in Mayo. A gentleman from Ohio owned it and never came to do anything on it. We had tried to purchase this property from him numerous times, but he would never agree to sell. Then, after we built our home on Long Lane, it came up for sale. The owner, Clement Meaux, was so overpriced it was out of the question. But now that it was in a realtor's hands, I thought, "Let's just call and inquire to see if the price has been lowered." It turns out that it had, and it was a lot cheaper than what we were originally quoted by the owner! I got excited and thought, "Maybe my husband will agree it's in a better range now, and we could try to get the money to buy it!" We ended up putting a contract on it and buying this property, the property I had wanted since I was just a young girl!

My husband had always dreamed of going into some type of business for himself. He can do just about anything, and I mean it when I say that! He built two of our homes — he can do it all when it comes to that! He's run all kinds of equipment, just about anything you can think of. Even if he doesn't know how, he will at least try it. We pondered starting a gutter and construction business. He has always done construction work on the side of his public jobs. We added in gutter installation and began the business in 2016. It has been very successful in our small hometown.

I, too, have always wanted to own my own business. I started one in 2005 on Indian Creek Road, and ran it out of a small building we built where we built our first home. It was called Country at Heart Gift Store. I sold primitives and candles there. Considering it was located in the country, a good mile off a dead-end road, it did fairly well. A year later, I ended up closing it, because I felt like I no longer wanted to do it. I am also the owner of a little online business called Eweniquely Kentucky. I began that business in October of 2016. I mainly just sell items from Facebook and at events. But in the last few months, I've not worked on it as much as I did in the beginning phase of the business, although I've done quite well.

In the summer of 2017, I considered writing my own book about my life. I started, but took a break after only a couple months. I had my sights set on the B&S Store that was no longer in operation, after having closed in 2009. I was also in the beginning works of opening my Eweniquely Kentucky store in Danville, Kentucky. After discussing things with my husband, we both agreed upon going the route of opening the old historic B&S Store of Mayo. We felt this would better serve the community. These old country stores had already served for well over one hundred years. The task has not been easy, and, at times, daunting and overwhelming, but, with faith and perseverance, it's happening.

I'll never forget when we first got the store, we went into our insurance agency to put insurance on it. The first thing he said was that it was in too bad of shape! Now, if only he had told me this a few years ago, to the same girl who let the negative thoughts affect her decisions to open Don Grey's other country store in Mayo. I would've thrown in the towel, right then and there. But I had grown from that time in 2008 to even now, in 2018. By that, I mean I had learned to not listen to my negative thoughts or the negative opinion others may hold. Instead, I learned to grow and look at the positives. Initially, those words from the insurance agent, almost had the effect it used to, but I bounced right back from that by seeing what I believe in.

All that really mattered was that I had a dream and a vision for this store! Yes, it was a mess! A complete mess of years and years' worth of trash and clutter and neglect. In my eyes, I saw hope and beauty through its ashes. After we cleaned and cleaned some more and decluttered, getting rid of all the trash, it was in pretty good shape, considering its age. Sure, it needed minor repairs, just like a home would.

Today, I'm stepping out of my comfort zone and into my dreams and visions. Don't let negativity from yourself or others, hold you back for as long as I did. It accomplishes nothing! Instead, it holds you in bondage to it! With a dream, a vision, and a plan, you can achieve anything you want! Don't give up, because there will be many road blocks ahead. Stay focused on the positive and go full steam ahead! Consider famous people, like Walt Disney. He was fired from the Kansas City Star in 1919, because the editor said he lacked imagination and had no good ideas. Now, can you imagine that? He didn't give up or throw in the towel because of the negative. He obviously tried and tried again! It was said that he was turned down three hundred times before finally getting the financing for his dream of Walt Disney World! Now, since he never gave up, he is regarded as one of the most creative men of the 20th century.

Colonel Sanders, of KFC Kentucky Fried Chicken, was rejected 1,009 times before anyone accepted his idea. He didn't give up! Could you imagine just being told "no" or your idea being rejected, not once, but 1,009 times? Wow! That is some perseverance of not giving in to negativity or rejection! He went on to create one of the largest fast food chains in the world. He didn't let negative people or the word "no" defeat him. When he died, he had an estimated worth of 3.5 million dollars! He opened his first KFC franchise at the age of 64. His company, KFC, has an estimated net worth of 15 billion dollars, as of 2013. Just think: if he gave up after the first rejection, he would have never have started a fast food empire. He didn't give up!

Elvis Presley is a musical legend. A musician Elvis auditioned for advised him to stick to driving a truck, telling him he would never make it as a singer! We already know he didn't let that guy's words hold him back. Many people will have opinions, some of which might even be harsh. Rise above them, and go out on a limb. If you are turned down, or fall, get right back up and try, try again!

History of OLD STORES

The old-time general stores were a symbol of American Enterprise. Almost forgotten in today's world, the old-fashioned general country stores could be found in every community, every corner, and every crossroad in the 19th and 20th centuries. They carried just about everything, from small needs in the home to large needs for farming. In the days of the general stores, almost everything came in bulk. Most everything was sold for cash, the only exceptions were what was traded for eggs, butter, or milk. Only credit was extended to those who were considered "most trustworthy", but, in those days, you could take a man's word to the bank. You would find anything from material being sold for women to make their own clothes with, or any tools, hoe, axes, hammers, or nuts and bolts. Cooking materials, such as flour, sugar, lard, and molasses mostly came in bulk, because everyone cooked in those days. They also raised their food, such as gardens, orchards, berries, and raising of livestock. The shelves were stocked with cleaning supplies, dental hygiene products, liniments for sore muscles, iodine for cuts, and other helpful medicinal products. Most prosperity of the old general stores were between the 1820s and 1850s. They updated their displays with much nicer glass displays for their merchandise.

Many country general stores remained an important asset for the goods and served as a gathering place in the community they were located in. Usually, these stores were heated with a large, potbellied stove, right in the center of the room. Most who gathered to talk around the stove or chat would play rook or checkers.

In the community of Mayo, there is a house that stands almost in front of the Mayo Christian Church that a man in our community grew up in. It was a tall gate house. The fee, if walking, was five cents. If by horse and buggy, ten cents. These were common in the 1800s and phased out by 1900. His father lived there, and he was born in that home. John Meaux was a wealthy plantation owner who moved from Virginia to Mayo, Kentucky in 1784, bringing with him sixty of his slaves. He owned a lot of Central Pike and Indian Creek Road. Between 1801 and 1802, he acquired 115 additional acres. His total land ownership in 1810 had increased to a sum of 1,851 acres. It was obvious that John Meaux had moved his plantation-style farming operation to Mercer County. The proximity of his land to the Kentucky River afforded him the opportunity to sell his crops in markets along the Kentucky, Ohio, and Mississippi rivers, all the way to the New Orleans. He was a very wealthy man. All his land, horses, mares, mules, and colts were valued at $32,500.

On October 23, 1826, John Meaux made his last will and testament. First, he directed all the slaves be forever emancipated and set free, totaling 61 in number. He further directed his executors, John G. Meaux and Nathanial B. Meaux, and his friend John B. Thompson, to "bound out" out the younger slaves to trades, all except for ten cows and ten ewes for each of his grandsons, John Woodson Meaux and Richard Meaux. He directed the remaining stock, crops, and plantation tools and utensils to be "divided among his negroes, hereby emancipated." He also directed his executors "to sell the land I purchased of Edwards" — that had not been previously "conveyed away" — as soon as the title was settled. All household and kitchen furniture was ordered to be sold. The proceeds from all the sales were applied by the executors, to the use of his slaves. The slaves were able to leave to any free state, like Indiana or Ohio. The John Meaux property division in 1837, and subsequent deeds, indicate most of the former slaves opted to stay in Mercer County, rather that move to another free state. The inventory and appraisement of the estate of John Meaux, dated February 9, 1830, excluding the value of the emancipated slaves, was $2,131.0075. It was not what he had done while living that defined John Meaux, but rather, it was what he did after his death, that separated him from other plantation owners of his time.

The John Meaux property included most of Central Pike and the east and west sides of Indian Creek Road. Certain landmarks along Central Pike, near Mayo, confirm the surveyor's placement of the property owned by the slaves. The Dividing Ridge Church, Meaux AME Chapel was established in 1870. Many descendants of the slaves still live in Mercer County. Many still own land in Mayo, Central Pike, and Indian Creek Road, where I live now. Our home on Indian Creek, which was part of the plantation acreage John Meaux owned from the 1700s to 1800s, has an old log barn that joins us and set on the Meaux property, dating back to the 1800s to 1830s. Clement Meaux owned the land I live on now, and his mother, Mrs. Meaux, owned my neighbor's property. The land we owned on Central Pike was also owned by John Meaux.

When we put our home on that piece of land, where we were digging the footers, we uncovered many broken dishes underground. We found beautiful pottery and all different colors of glassware in shades of pink and blue, tiny pieces of dishes with birds on them and other beautiful designs. We also found crock marble, shoe buckles, and thimbles. When my husband was pushing around dirt from what looked to be a cellar, we found an old, small, unbroken bottle called Calder's Dentine, used for teeth. We also found an old skeleton key and burnt bricks on the property. When we asked around, no one— not even the older guy in his seventies or early eighties who owned B&S Store at the time— remembered a home being there, but there was lots of evidence pointing to a home being there previously, long before, probably early in the 1900s. I'm sure it belonged to John Meaux, or his slaves, or maybe even family members.

Meaux was buried in Providence Presbyterian Church Cemetery (1734-1828). His name also appears on a plaque at the Old Fort Cemetery, in Harrodsburg. The plaque shows those who served in the Revolutionary War and were laid to rest in Mercer County, Kentucky. I find it neat that I've owned property — well, two properties, to be exact — that once was in his plat he owned. Also, that the property on Central Pike that we owned was in with the store we bought at one time and later divided off from the store.

My mom purchased a little country store in Terrapin, just about a mile from the store I currently own, which I have named Vickie's Mayo Country Store and Cafe. It was located at the four-way stop intersection, just past Indian Creek Road. The four-way intersection joins Vanardsdall Road, Kirkwood Road, and 1160 Talmage-Mayo Road. It set right next to the road where Talmage-Mayo Road joined up with the other two roads. She purchased this store sometime in the early 80s, and she said someone stopped and was talking with her and suggested she name it "Terrapin Variety Store." So, that's exactly what she did! It had a variety of things, just like the name said. Just about anything you could think of, from jewelry to guns, to clothes, to food and drinks. She ran it for a couple of years and later sold it. It sat empty for years afterwards. It no longer stands today. It was either burned or torn down, like so many other old stores in our state.

Thomas Shelton was nicknamed "Tommy Terp", giving Terrapin its name. When Shelton was a child, he showed his playmates a nest of terrapin eggs he had found, and, from then on, they called him Terrapin. He grew up to be a rural mail carrier in a one-horse spring wagon, haul freight, and run the general store at the crossroads between Mayo-Kirkwood, Duganville, and St. Pike, now Vanarsdall Road. The place was named Terrapin for him.

The Road to My Old Kentucky Home

There was another man named John Royalty, who lived there and tried to change the name to Royalty's Crossroads, but failed. He ran the store there later and bought it from Tommy Terp. Neighbors said, "You can call it what you darn well please, but it will always be 'Terrapin' to us." Another two and a half to three miles on down, on 1160 Talmage-Mayo, in Duganville, is another store that is still standing today. Duganville Store is a two-story structure, sitting right next to the road, almost on the road, at the crossroads to Bethel Road and Stratton Road. It was operated in the 1900s by Demaree and Norton. Years later, it was owned by the masonic lodge. A dark building that joined the store is no longer attached, but it can still be seen in pictures. The road is right next to the white store now.

There is also a store on the crossroads from Central Pike to 390 Bohon Road, called Duncan. An act to establish the town of Duncansville was approved December 2, 1851. The road leading from Harrodsburg to Bloomfield crosses said road. Here is a picture of The Duncan Store in 1915 with horses and buggies lined up in front of it.

Group At Duncan Store (About 1900)

This photo owned by Mrs. Sallie Reed, Louisville, shows a group at Duncan store about 1900. This building, owned by John E. Sims, later burned, Mrs. Reed says. Pictured, front row, left to right, the boys are sons of Henry Hendren, Worley Graham, Bill Voorhies, Henry Hendren, not named, Claude Ransdell, and Sam Graham. Second row, left to right, Joe Sims, (next man not known), S. Ransdell, Ira Taylor, Harve Lake, Clyde Hendren, Vanetti Brown, Claude Sims, Simp. Hendren, Jim Hendren, and a Mr. Watts.

Back row, from left to right, Hess Carnic, Harve Rose, John E. Sims, Henry Sims, Creed Rose, Arnold Johnson, Price (Bock) Pinkston, Vaulter Graham, Ebb Million, John Reed, John Taylor, Moss Cunningham, Hansford Sims, Elijah Reed, and Sam Voorhies.

The other is the group at the Duncan Store about 1900.

There was another store about three miles down from Duncan Store, called the Tablow Store. It was settled beside Bethel Baptist Church. Many folks reported going over to the store on Wednesday nights — as soon as church let out — to get pickled bologna and crackers and soda for ten cents. It seems the kind of stories you hear from the days when there were little country stores on almost every corner no longer exist. These were good times, good memories — the good ole days! Many people recount the fun they had and fond memories of this era. Memories of playing checkers or playing rook, gathered close to a wood-burning stove, with laughter, storytelling, and jokes. The memories that are in our minds we hold dear and are forever grateful for them. To have experienced these days and years that are now gone, memories only serve to remind us of these days gone by, but not forgotten. I have learned so much.

The Road to My Old Kentucky Home

I was born in the mid-70s, so I have gotten to experience what my children got to, for a few, very short years, of their lives. By the time my children came along in the mid to late 90s, most communities had already closed the doors to these stores. It is sad they are really only history and a memory now.

A social media post I created for my online store, said:

> *You know, I remember when we were trying to get insurance on the store. We were buying, and it was around three to four months before they could find a company to insure it. I almost gave up on it. They had tried several companies at Farm Bureau, who they work with to insure it, until finally, after trying and trying, they found a company willing. I asked the owner of my insurance company why he told me he wasn't sure I was going to find a company that would. He said the place was in bad shape. In his voice, you could tell he wasn't sure if they could find one to insure it. I got to thinking maybe the store was in too bad of shape, too. In a way, it was. But all I could see was the beauty in the ashes. Its potential, the dreams I had for it. He was very skeptical and made me start to wonder if there was any use. But I'd like to use this as my "how many times habe people looked at us and given up hope for us or labeled us as beyond repair? You know, just as I envision a dream for this place to be restored to its beauty, I see beauty beyond the mountains of garbage and clutter and years of neglect. But you know...God sees us the same way when we feel broken, unusable, or unrestorable...God sees us in our best. The best He has created us for!!! Achievers, overcomers, dreamers. He gives us beauty for the ashes.*

I was one of the most bashful and shy people I knew. I always got embarrassed very easily, it seemed. I remember in school, I would rather have taken an "F" on a subject then to get up and give an oral report! I was always quiet, so it was hard for me to make friends. I remember hating to get up and walk in front of people, especially if I had to walk alone or up in front of a room. Sounds crazy, I know! Even on my wedding day, I didn't want it too big. I said, "I don't want all those people looking at me!" We married in the church Johnnie and I grew up in together, as kids. His cousin, the pastor of Free Pentecostal in Willisburg, Kentucky, married us with only two witnesses (his mom and dad)! I was so shy, I said, "I don't want any more!"

Now that I look back, I wish I had let my parents come to our wedding. The things you do when you're young! I look back now and feel so different, and, now, would make a different decision. In my years of growing up, it just never felt like I had a great deal of self-esteem, which carried into my adult life. It does have an impact on your life—no doubt about that!

One day, I went to a service just for ladies at Harrodsburg Church of God, and I had a woman speak into my life. She said I was somebody and that I was not inferior to other people! I was shocked, but I knew the Lord had spoken to her, because I had never seen this woman before! Sadly, this was true for my life. For some reason, when I was growing up, I always put people above me and felt beneath them, like I could never measure up to their standards. After this lady's words, I felt like I was slowly coming out of this mindset and my shyness, as bad as it was.

I took on a class at Harrodsburg Church of God and started teaching a teen class. I remember when I first took on this class, the ages ranged from thirteen to nineteen years old. I was very intimidated and had never done a group with these ages. I was very nervous on my first Sunday school class day. Before long, I was getting a lot more confidence and wasn't as nervous teaching, as I once was. We had so much fun! Johnnie came to my class, usually to support me. We would do fun activities outside of church with the class, from four-wheeling, to swimming, to field trips to Mammoth Cave, to movies, to cookouts, to lock-ins at the church.

From there, I started a choir at our church and it did so well we had half the church participating in it. Then, I started playing the piano for church, in place of our pastor's wife. She had cancer and couldn't play like she had before. I took her place and played and sang for about three years. I was finally coming out of my shyness.

One day, I was asked to fill in for my oldest brother and teach the adult Sunday school class. I kindly turned the man who was asking me down, telling him he would be a lot better for the job than I was! He laughed and said, "Now he (my older brother) didn't ask me—he asked you!" I thought about it later and decided I would. Even though I was nervous, I made it through! Later, I was asked more often to teach the adult class, and, over time, it became easier for me to do.

Now, remember, in school, I would rather have taken an "F" than to get up and give an oral speech. Somehow, after help from the Lord had been spoken, I got a lot better with it. Sure, I would still get nervous, but I had gone from not wanting to be in school to enjoying teaching an adult class at church!

I'd like to leave a few passages from the Bible here:

> *Philippians 4:6-8 (KJV): Be careful for nothing; but in everything by prayer and supplication, with thanksgiving let your requests be made known unto God. And the Peace of God, which passeth all understanding, shall keep your hearts and minds through Christ Jesus. Finally brethren, whatsoever things are true, whatsoever things are honest, whatsoever things are just, whatsoever things are pure, whatsoever things are lovely, whatsoever things are of good report, if there be any virtue, and if there be any praise, think on these things.*
>
> *Proverbs 23:7 (KJV): For as he thinketh in his heart, so is he.*
>
> *Proverbs 4:23 (KJV): Keep thy heart with all diligence; for out of it are the issues of life.*

Doing as these words has helped me in my life. They have helped me to be an overcomer in the areas of shyness, self-doubt, and no confidence. These words have been a light to my path. I believe our words or thoughts can have life or be death to us, like Proverbs 18:21 (KJV), "Death and life are in the power of the tongue." When the opportunity to open the store came to me, I actually spoke the words out loud to myself. My tongue said, "You can't do that. \You don't have enough experience," and I listened to the negative words. If I would have believed in myself and spoke life and positivity, it would've turned out much different. I had the opportunity to go to the Cane Ridge meeting house a couple years ago, in 2016. It was a very neat place to go to learn the history of our forefathers here in the state of Kentucky. It's located in Bourbon County, a little over an hour away from Harrodsburg, near Paris, Kentucky. The Ridge was named by the explorer Daniel Boone, who noticed a form of bamboo growing there. The 1791 Cane Ridge meeting house is believed to be the longest single room log structure in North America.

Revival broke out at Cane Ridge in August of 1801. Wagon carriages came along the narrow roads. Hundreds of men, women, and children came to Cane Ridge Church, about twenty miles east of Lexington, Kentucky. They partook of communion. The news set the most populous region of the state on fire. People poured in by the thousands! One traveler wrote a friend. He was on his way to the greatest meeting of its kind, even now. He wrote, "I doubt not, but there will be ten thousand people." Three to five-day meetings climaxed. With the communion, people gathered in the dozens. Hundreds at Cane Ridge. Sometimes, 20,000 people came on the grounds! Watching, praying, preaching, weeping, groaning, and falling. Though some stood at the edge and mocked, most left marveled at the awesome hand of God. Cane Ridge quickly became one of the best reported events and most important religious gatherings of all American history. For decades, the prayer of camp meeting and revivals everywhere was, "Lord make it like Cane Ridge."

The event was led by 18 Presbyterian ministers and numerous Methodist and Baptist preachers. We got the privilege to go in with my church, and we had a little service in that building from 1791. It was a very neat experience. We sang some hymns and had some devotions. There, where it all happened, the Great Revival of Cane Ridge.

The Road to My Old Kentucky Home

We have so much rich history here in Kentucky, especially in Harrodsburg. The history of the Old Mud Meeting House in Mercer County goes back over 400 years from Holland, to New York, to New Jersey, to Pennsylvania, and, finally, to Kentucky! Members of this Dutch reformed congregation immigrated to Kentucky as early as 1781. Many pioneers rest in the cemetery located beside the Old Mud Meeting House. Revolutionary soldiers are among the buried there. A colony of immigrants from Holland made their way to Kentucky in the 18th century, arriving in Mercer County with their customs. They had a distinctive building technique.

The Synod of the Dutch Reformed Church sent Rev. Peter Labaugh to Harrodsburg in 1796 to establish a church. He returned to Jersey to raise the funds to purchase land in Mercer County where the Mud Meeting House now stands. He bought the site on Dry Branch Road, the site on Dry Fork of Salt River, from David and Elizabeth Adams. The Dutch migrants built the Old Mud Meeting House in 1800, on limestone foundation with exposed vertical timbers. The dimensions were 46.4 x 34.4. It has sixteen roof trusses. The church featured hand-hewn heavy timber framework. Mortise and tenor joiner, wattle and daub walls. This technique is used in several homes of Mercer County residents of the same period. It is the first Dutch Reformed Church built west of the Alleghenies. It's constructed of sturdy oak timbers and the walls were filled with mud mixed with straw and sticks, hence, its name, the Old Mud Meeting House. The first pastor of the church was Donnie Thomas Kyle, and he is buried in the old graveyard next to the church.

Graham Springs and Hotel, which was a spring like that of Tatham Springs, was located in Harrodsburg, Kentucky. It was built in 1819, by Dr. C.C. Graham, who owned it for thirty years. To talk to him was a treat! He knew Daniel Boone and George Rogers Clark. He witnessed Indian fights and served in the war of 1812 and the Black Hawk War. He had all sorts of interesting experiences to tell. 10,000 people came to celebrate the 66th anniversary of the founding of Harrodsburg, the first permanent settlement in Kentucky in 1841. There were 15,000 ladies in the crowd and ten military companies. One woman described what she remembered as a little girl of Graham Springs: long porties with great white columns up to the roof, where the beaux and belles walked up and down in what seemed a fairy procession. The ladies with their beautiful, elaborately dressed hair, true to New Orleans fashion. In a letter to her aunt, written from the Springs on July 27, 1829, she says,

> *Oh, if I could only describe to you this lovely place. The many comforts and luxuries we have here, together with the interesting gentlemen. Very few young ladies besides ourselves, at present, and so many elegant gentlemen — you see, we are belles of necessity. There are two gentlemen worth more than a million apiece. Both quite interesting, and there are drivers. Others more talented, but not so brilliant. The table is the best I have ever seen sat down to at any place. Ice cream in profusion, the cottages are finished prettily, all of them with large closets. A splendid band and a stand in the yard overlooking the whole place. And the band stationed up here. Before daybreak, you are awakened by delightful music which continues until night. Then, it is removed to a most splendid ballroom, where you enter dazzled by glittering lights and interesting company. I have not powers of description to describe to you one half the beauties of this lovely place. I have visited nearly all the watering places in Virginia, but I do not think any of them half as delightful. There are daily arrivals of gentlemen, a great many from Tennessee and South Carolina and the interior of Kentucky. There are five baths for ladies and gentlemen. And I have said nothing of the ten-pin ally and many other things of interest to amuse you. The facilities are provided for those and amusements which seem necessary at such a place to dispel monotony. There were some playing chess or backgammon, some throwing the hoop, others engaged at battle down the ten pins.*

Many people went to the springs for more pleasure than health. As a constant visitor put it, the water was nasty and strong enough to nauseate one. It did no good. The prings were the grand summer rallying ground for Southern belles and beaux. It was the place of romance and flirtation. Graham Springs was called the Saratoga of the South. The guest register for 1835-1836 shows the largest number of visitors. From New Orleans, to Natchez, to Vicksburg, to Nashville, to New York, people flocked from across the country. The Clays, Brekin Ridge, Isaac Shelby, and many other well-known, prominent names from our own state frequented Graham Springs. It was a combined place of pleasure and fun and a health resort.

Graham Springs of 1830s and 1840s. Doctor Christopher Columbus Graham, C.C. Graham, around on the buildings and grounds, probably one half million dollars. Now, that would equal somewhere between five and seven million dollars. This fascinating era extended to 1853, giving Harrodsburg the name as Health Center of the South and Saratoga of the West.

The Greenville Springs was about a half mile away from Graham Springs. When Greenville Springs was popular, it could accommodate 300 guests and stables for their horse carriages. Accommodations for 300 guests meant the hotel was quite large for those days, but it was soon overtaken by the large Graham Springs, in 1827. He purchased the 207 acres that comprised the Greenville Springs property. The next year, another 60 or 70 acres that included Harrodsburg or Suttons Springs. The estate totaled nearly 300 acres. He took his servants to the Kentucky River, where they cut timbers for boats and loaded them with all kinds of shrubbery from the area. He brought them to the Graham Springs to line the walkways and landscape. To these, they added exotics from Europe and Asia.

In June 1853, Graham Springs was sold to the federal government to be an old soldier's home. It burned in 1856. It is now the home of James B. Haggin Memorial Hospital, which was established 1913.

I could only imagine living in those days and seeing all the beauty and splendor of Graham Springs, Greenville Springs, or Tatham Springs! To see what it was like to get to be invited to one of the balls they had. To see the architecture of that time, especially the Graham Springs. The beautiful gardens and exotic shrubs and flowers. The Southern belles and beaux in their fancy attire. To go back to a simpler time. A time when worked at home, rather than going to a job every day. Sure, they had plenty of work at home, mostly raising children and taking care of the home and doing the chores around the house. A time when people and families actually spent time talking and engaging with one another playing cards and checkers.

Many of whom I've spoken to mention openly that the "good ole days" were in the early 1900s. They talk and reminisce about being with family, going to Sunday school, going to meetings, and helping one another out. It was a time when a handshake was as good as a man's word; it really was a contract by today's standards. It was a time when everyone in small towns and communities knew one another and lent a helping hand when one was in need and returned the favor and kept their end of the bargain, so to speak. It was a time when families spent time around the tables talking and listening to one another, and people had values and morals and most folks went to church. When old general stores were on every corner.

People respected one another, and children respected their elders, or they'd get a spanking. The spankings were not beatings—in fact, I remember a few spankings I got that I actually needed. I remember when paddling was allowed in school, and our whole class— all thirty-two of us— got paddled by our teacher just for one classmate getting us all in trouble. It never hurt any one of us. It may have hurt our feelings, but we needed it, and we actually respected her more for it!

I'd love to go back in time! I always said I should have been born in the 1930s or 1940s. I love vehicles from that era. I'd love to live in a time when televisions weren't ramped in every home, and most children had their chores to do. There weren't kids hooked on drugs or rebellion. Most of the time, a good spanking would take care of that kind of thing.

Nowadays, you have building codes for everything. I know the B&S Store never had railings all the way across their porch and spindles, and the potbellied stoves were okay. Ponds were unfenced. Now, everything is regulated for safety. It used to be that parents just told your kids not to touch it or go around it, and they listened!

To go back, to sit on the porches and talk with friends, family, and neighbors or after Sunday church was over, and coming home, eating dinner, and sitting around the big oak trees in the yards on a hot sunny day, enjoying the shade and any breezes that blow your way. I can hear the sound of laughter and children laughing, running, playing hide and seek, or playing dodgeball. Or in the summer, at dusk, catching lightning bugs and putting them in a jar, cutting holes in the lid, so they can get air. Going fishing or swimming in creeks. My childhood included some of this, and they were the best times!

I remember going to Randall Burns Store with my childhood friend on summer break. Back then, you could go inside stores barefooted. A lot of folks did in those general stores. When the times started to change in the late 70s and 80s, they would post a sign on the door stating, "No shirt, no shoes, no service." The "no shirt", of course, referred to men, because you never had to worry about women not wearing a shirt—ladies were much more modest in those days.

Back then, you could play outside for hours! I'd play in the fields with my brother and his friend, never having to worry about someone trying to kidnap or hurt us. Our parents felt safe not checking on us for a few hours at a time. It was a more innocent time.

Most churches and stores had outhouses and no running water— only wells! When riding in the car with your mom, you didn't have car seats or seat belts. If you were riding upfront when your mom had to throw on the brakes, her arm was your seatbelt! She'd throw her arm across your chest, just like a seatbelt. As a child, I didn't get everything I wanted, and I am more grateful for the things I did get. For Christmas, we would get fruit and nuts, maybe one toy. These days, most kids would laugh in your face or ask, "What is this?" if that's all they got for Christmas—my own children included! But I *did* get love from my parents, and that meant more than any gift I could've gotten.

I remember when my friend and I would ride bikes down steep hills on the Indian Creek Road without my parents there to make sure we didn't wreck. But, guess what? We were just fine! One day when I was 11, my sister-in-law and I rode our bikes to Mayo Store. Mind you, I was the baby of six kids. She had married my oldest brother, who is fourteen years my senior. We went to get some sodas at the store. When we left Don Grey's store, I had to ride past B&S on my way back home. As I was getting right in front of B&S, I wrecked! I got too close to the edge of the road and went over the bank! I was laying there with my feet straight up in the air, and there sat a few farmers laughing on the front porch. Talk about embarrassing—man alive!

I've had the honor of seeing one of the last standing Hotel and Spas of the 19th Century. I didn't get to see it in its glory days, but it sure looked glorious to me! It looked like a mansion. It was a humongous building of some sort! Structurally, it had very unique architecture. My husband recounts how when he was younger, and no one was in the old Tatham Hotel Springs and Spa, he and his four brothers would sneak around and play hide and seek. He said they would run all over the land and sneak into the swimming pool, out back. They got run off the property.

As kids growing up in the 70s, 80s, and 90s, we'd play in the woods for hours. We'd build forts or huts or treehouses all day. We never got in trouble for being gone too long. It was a great time to be a kid!

When I was a kid, Harrodsburg had a drive-in theater called Twin Hills. It sat on one little hill, and, past the huge movie screen that stood about thirty feet in the air, was another hill that resembled the first one. Hence the name, Twin Hills Drive-In. It opened in 1961. There was a little concession stand in the center of the property, which also had a manager's office located in it. The movie sound was transmitted to radios on stands, where you parked your vehicle. It was a fun, family outing to go see these large-screen movies, where you could sit outside in your fold-up chairs or blankets, eating your goodies from the concession stand. The theater was across the street from a huge farm that grew corn.

When I was around 10, I went to the drive-in with my older siblings, and the movie playing was *Children of the Corn*. It was kind of a scary movie for my age. The friend who had come with me was two years younger than I was, so it must have been even scarier for her. We were sitting across the street from acres and acres of corn. It kind of made me paranoid, since we literally had a corn field next to us!

The classic-style drive-in reopened in 2005. I took my own children to Twin Hills Drive-In after it reopened. It ran until 2016, when it was demolished to make way for storage units. The first-ever drive-in theater was born in 1933 on Crescent Boulevard in Camden, New Jersey. The idea caught on, and, when Hollinghead's patent was overturned in 1949, drive-in theaters began popping up all over the country.

I remember a covered bridge in Washington County, Kentucky that I saw when I was younger. I always loved to get out and ride on country roads and take little backroad trips— as I like to call them. Backroad trips are a great way to enjoy the changing seasons in the spring and autumn and the weather in the summer. The road bypassed beside the covered bridge, because it was no longer safe for vehicles to pass over it. It's said there was a lot of vandalism inside the bridge.

Mooresville Covered Bridge.

In the 80s, there seemed to be a lot more vandalism than in previous years. They had done some repairs to the bridge formerly known as Beech Fork Covered Bridge. Now it's mostly known as Mooresville Covered Bridge. It sits over the Beech Fork River in Washington County, Kentucky. The bridge was used until around 1975 when a concrete bridge was built a little way up from the bridge. The old covered bridge was built sometime around the 1860s. Most old covered bridges were built in the 1800s or early 1900s. The work and craftsmanship that went into these covered bridges are nothing like the ones built today. Lots of hard work went into construction of covered bridges.

I worked at Shaker Village in Harrodsburg, in the 2000s. I worked in housekeeping at the time, and we had to clean a lot of historic buildings that line the village scenery. It's one of the most beautiful places in Mercer County. The long road that is there now was once the main road to Lexington. Beautiful, large sugar maples line each side of the road. The huge buildings look like mansions. When I had to go in these and clean the rooms people had rented for their vacation stay at the Village, I could admire the craftsmanship of the builders in every area of the buildings. From the foundation to the roof, from the flooring to the and trim and windows of every single building they built.

Shaker Village was home to Pleasant Hill Shakers. They were recognized for their iconic architecture, skilled craftsmanship, and spirituality. Over a 105-year timespan, they constructed over 260 structures on the property. Most of the structures are built with limestone from the Kentucky River. The structures are as sound today as they were when they were built, over 200 years ago. The Shaker brand is known far and wide for its excellence.

In the 1830s, Shaker Village was a thriving community of 500 people, spread over 4,000 acres. In 1923, the last Shaker died, and Pleasant Hill remained empty. Sometime in the 1960s, restoration began, and preservation started. 34 buildings have been restored, and the Shaker Village farmland has been preserved.

While employed there, I heard all kinds of stories about the Shakers. I decided to go to my local library in Mercer County to find out more for myself. I found several books on the Shaker Village of Pleasant Hill, and I checked them all out and began reading up on the Shakers of Pleasant Hill. Quickly, one young man stood out to me in amazement. Micajah Burnett came here in 1809 with his parents when he was 17 years old. He began to lay out the Village, the Meetinghouse, the barns, the craft shops, and the dwellings. He used the materials that were available and followed the architecture of the Mt. Lebanon

Ministry. He knew the federal style that Shakers knew. To me, what seemed so beautiful was the winding staircase at the Trustees Building. The beauty of the architecture, wood, and detail is amazing. The twin staircases that wind up to the top floor, and the beauty of looking down from the top to the bottom floor is truly indescribable! This was an unusual style of architectural design. He had no advanced tools of the day to work with to bed the rails of wood up the three flights of steps. The wood is a gorgeous Cherrywood, rich in color. Although I am no longer employed there, I still love to visit throughout the year. It feels as though you've stepped back in time, to the days when the Shakers lived there.

So much history lies in Harrodsburg, which is called the "City of Firsts". Established June 16, 1774, Harrodsburg is the oldest settlement west of the Allegheny Mountains. From the Old Fort, Greenville Springs, Harrodsburg/Graham Springs, offered mineral water, gambling, and horse racing. Abraham Lincoln's parents were married in the crude log cabin in 1806. The Old Mud Meeting House was the first Dutch Reformed Church west of the Allegheny Mountains. Mercer County Fair and Horse Show has been in operation every summer since 1828. It's thought to be the oldest running fair in America. It is also home to the oldest taverns in Kentucky. Harrodsburg had its own buggy factory called the Bohon Buggy, the D.T. Bohon Company of Harrodsburg, Kentucky.

Bohon Buggy Company in Harrodsburg, Kentucky in the 1920s

Bottom's Bluegrass Buggies from factory to you. The famous vehicle factory, covering six acres, located in Harrodsburg, Kentucky.

It was the largest exclusive vehicle factory in the world! D.T. Bohon was born in Harrodsburg, Kentucky in 1878 and died a sudden death from complications of pneumonia. At just 44 years old, it was very unexpected. His buggies were sold and shipped all over the world. People wrote reviews of the buggies they had purchased from him. They all talked about how stylish they were, the compliments they received from neighbors, the comfort of riding in one, and the value of it at a good price.

In the *Climax-Madisonian* paper, April 14, 1915, an ad reads: *Kentucky made vehicles for Kentucky people at wholesale factory prices. Our large modern factory is just as up to date as any in the United States. We have every facility for manufacturing high-grade vehicles at the lowest cost of production. Please don't confuse our factory with some of the small repair shops here in Central Kentucky that possibly assemble one hundred vehicles a year. For we manufacture them by the thousands and sell them all over the United States as well as in many foreign countries. We have every new labor-saving machine, every practical arrangement known. We have here as fine a collection of vehicle builders as was ever gotten together by any firm, anywhere. They are men of experience and ability. Clean, moral and conscientious. They are men who like their work. Visit our factory and our office if you can, and see for yourself how Bohon vehicles are made. If every vehicle user in Kentucky really knew the truth and the facts about the wonderful values we give, despite our already tremendous business, we would have to increase our factory, at least, ten to fifteen times, to supply the demand. The large D.T. Bohon factory with annual capacity of 20,000 finished vehicles.*

In the early 1900s, the company produced 1,700 cars during its first full year of business. At the beginning of the 1900s, the automobile entered the transportation market as a "toy" for the rich. Henry Ford produced the Model T car for the average American, and, in 1920, Ford sold over a million cars. It wasn't until the 1930s and 1940s that more people could afford cars. A lady from Mayo in her 80s told me that when she was young, you just didn't go to town very much, because you had gardens, and you had chickens or pigs for your meat. In those days, she said, it may be once a month you travelled to town. Most only had horses. Some had horses and wagons. Some, who were a little wealthier, had buggies like that of the Bohon Buggies. Only the very wealthy had cars.

A newspaper clipping from June of 1900 about the little community of Mayo:

Mayo...we are a most industrious and enterprising village in Mercer County. We have the same conveniences here in Mayo that people have in large towns, such as groceries, dry goods, stores, mills, two blacksmith shops and a woodwork shop. We also have churches, both white and colored, and the large cities cannot beat us for gas. We have a gas plant, known as I.D.C. Gas Company.

The Mayo community was formerly known as Mayo Village. In the past, Mayo was a very busy community full of friends and families that came there to do their weekly trading and catch up on all the news. Some have suggested Mayo was named after Dr. James Mayo, but no one knows how it got its name for sure. In 1870, African-Americans built the Dividing Ridge Baptist Church on the same property at which it stands now. They also built a school known as Mayo School. In the early 1900s, the Union Missionary Church stood where Hopewell Baptist Church now stands. The church had four denominations: Methodist, Christian, Baptist, and Presbyterian. The churches would all rotate Sundays. It also served as a school. Most of Mayo's children went to school there.

In 1903, a committee was appointed to build a Christian Church. Van Carter, a previous owner of Mayo General Store, donated the land that once was joined to the General Store for the church to build on.

Old Hillsboro Church I attended as a young girl in Washington County. Where I got saved at when I was eight years old

Mt. Olivet Baptist Church in Tatham

Wash Johnson, father of Con Johnson and grandfather to Wendall Johnson, was very involved in getting the church started. He helped in getting it organized, he helped financially, and he and his sons contributed lumber from their farm and helped in the building of the church. The church was completed in 1905. Reverend O.J. Young gave the dedication sermon. There have been several additions over the years, but the main worship room of the church remains the same as it did when it was originally built. In the 1920s, the Mayo Christian Church had summer Bible Schools and a singing school. The oldest grave in the cemetery of Mayo Christian Church is Wash Johnson, born 1838, died 1908. There are three churches in Mayo; The Mayo Christian Church, The Dividing Ridge Baptist Church (the church that shared Methodist, Baptist, and Presbyterian), and Union Missionary Church, which is now called Hopewell Baptist Church.

There were several schools in Mayo. Some were for the black community that lived there, and had a one room school next to the Dividing Ridge Baptist Church, and called Dividing

Ridge, which is built on land that John Meaux had owned and bought when he moved from Virginia and brought his slaves. In his will, he freed all his slaves and gave them part of his land, which was Central Pike and Indian Creek. Most of them owned this property now. Then there was the division of land that was between the Salt River and Chaplin River — how Dividing Ridge got its name. The school and church were on the corner of Central Pike and 1160 Talmage-Mayo Road in Mayo, next to Mayo General Store (owned then by A.R. Brown, who owned it from 1920s until 1979). Hopewell School was located at the Hopewell Baptist Church about a mile from Mayo. This was a one room school, as most were in 1929. Fairview School was a couple miles down the road in the opposite direction of Hopewell Baptist and Mayo. The earliest date of it was around 1938.

Fairview High School To Hold Reunion

e 22nd Annual Fairview School Reunion will be held at the Senior Citizens Center turday, Sept. 12, 1998 at 6:00 p.m. Pictured above is the class that would have ited from Fairview High School in 1948, but the school was reduced to a 10-year in 1946. The fourth grade class of 1939-1940 included : Back row (l-r) Ancil Yea- ford Taylor, Harold Gritton, Mrs. Opal Demaree (teacher), Roy E. Drury and M. Stratton. Middle row - Ralph Sanders, Jr., Benton Horn, James E. Riley, aye Pelly, C.W. Robinson and Lorraine Tackett. First row - Marvin Poulter, Sanders, Azille Satterly, Ida Mae Ashton, Rose Drury and Rosalyn Whi

48 | *The Road to My Old Kentucky Home*

Old Fairview School on 1160 Talmage Mayo Rd Mercer Ky
1930s, when it started operating as a school.

The Walker School in Terrapin area was opened in the 1930s. The Blossom School was located on Central Pike about three-and-a-half miles from Mayo. A new one was built sometime between 1920 and 1925.

There were two stores. The Mayo General Store that A.R. Brown owned—which people referred to as "The Brown's Store". This store had the first post office in Mayo, and Mr. Brown was the postman. In those days, most general stores had their own post office, and the store owners were postmasters. There was a blacksmith shop and garage that the Dickersons ran. The father, Bert, ran the blacksmith shop, and the son of Dorestus ran the garage. You could get your horses shod or "Tin Lizzie" repaired. In the 1920s, the Fort Model T was also knowns as a "Tin Lizzie".

The 1920s were known as "The Roaring 20s" because it was a time of noise, lively action, and economic prosperity. The First World War made American businesses rise. Factory production had sharply rose to meet the needs of the war. America had captured markets that had previously bought from Europe. Once the war was over, these countries continued buying American goods. The Republican presidents Harding, Coolidge, and Hoover tried to help American businesses. They increased taxation on foreign goods that came into the U.S., which was achieved by passing a new law called the Fordney-McCumber Tariff Act in 1922. These new taxes and tariffs made international goods more expensive to purchase, encouraging Americans to buy goods made in the U.S., leading to the boom of the 20s in America.

My grandmother, Dorothy Blanton Williams, was born in 1911, in Laurel County, Kentucky. Her father was George Blanton, and her mother was Sarah Noe. My grandmother and my grandfather, Glenn Williams, got married in London, Kentucky. They had eleven children; eight boys and three girls. They lived in London.

My mom's parents lived in Knox County, just a few miles down the road. My mom and dad got married in the early 60s, moving from their respective homes to Richmond, Kentucky, for a new job opportunity. In those days, the London area didn't have many job opportunities. It wasn't until they moved to Rose Hill, Kentucky (then Tatham and Willisburg), that we were born. I remember going to visit my grandparents and my cousins many times. My grandfather died a year before I was born, so I never got the chance to meet him.

My mom's father, Elmer Parker, died when I was five years old. I don't remember much about him, because didn't go to London often, as it was an hour-and-forty-five minute drive to London. I remember going to visit my grandmothers a lot more as I got older. It was always fun times. My grandma, Dora Parker, lived up on a hill. I recall there being bright orange clay dirt and lots of rocks exposed on that hill, with many pine trees. They are like cedars are here, in my home place of Harrodsburg.

I remember the coal in the shed piled high to heat her home and the awesome food she always prepared for us! She made the most delicious homemade biscuits I'd ever tasted! I always remember her tasty corn she froze from her garden every year. She was the best cook! Every time we ate, her food was incredibly delicious. I also remember the whole family sitting around in the living room telling stories. I remember many times looking off or looking at the TV and feeling someone staring at me. I'd turn around to look, and there she was, staring a hole through me. Our eyes would meet, and she would just smile real big at me. It felt like we lived so far away, and I always wished we lived closer, so we could visit more often and grow up with our cousins. The distance kept us away more than we liked. With jobs and everyday life, it was hard to go as much or as often as we wanted to.

My Grandma Williams and I were very close. When I was about fifteen years old, I went to stay with her for a week. I'll never forget the time we shared. She was only about four feet tall and wore her hair up high on her head—all of it white, except a little black strand right in front. She was one of the most positive people I ever knew.

She'd sit in her chair, looking out the window at her children and grandchildren who lived on the same road as her. Across the road from her, up the hill, sat her youngest child's home. She could see it in plain sight. She'd say, "There goes Clayton and Imogene!" Her son and daughter-in-law. Or, "There's Carl coming home!" It was fun to watch her and listen to her stories.

We would talk for hours, just her and I. I learned so much from her. She had a close walk with the Lord, and she lived out what she claimed to be. She was highly respected by people all over the community. She was a woman who was very strong in her Christian faith. She played the organ in church for years. She told me she went to church about five times a week! She visited other churches when her church didn't have a service.

I recall when I'd stay with her, we'd have pineapples from a can and cottage cheese—a lot! I grew to love it. Every time I eat it, I think of her and I sitting at the table, eating. She was one of the kindest people I've ever met, and her laugh was infectious! At many of our reunions and birthday parties, she was like a celebrity. People I didn't even know would try to talk to her, and it was hard to get time to talk with her, for all the other people attempting conversations with her. She lived to the ripe old age of 103. She passed away just one hour into her 104th birthday, on October 23, 2015. She is greatly missed, but she left a legacy behind to all who knew her. Most of the community called her "Grandma Williams." My grandmother was a great lady.

My roots run deep in London, Laurel, and Knox Counties. Both my mother's and father's side of the family live there. My third great-grandfather, Elder George Brock, on my dad's side of the family, was a very recognized and well-known man in Laurel. Elder was well known and recognized in the

Annals of Kentucky Baptist Ministry. Hannah Magee's history of the Durham family, states, George Brock was wonderfully familiar with scriptures and preached extensively in Laurel, Whitley, and Clay Counties. He was successful in leading many souls to Christ. He was truly devoted, a consecrated servant of God, loved and highly esteemed by his brethren. His convictions were fixed on the fundamental principles of the Gospel. In the history of the church of Laurel River Association, it reads, "He was very instrumental in establishing many churches in Laurel and nearby counties. From around late spring, or early summer, 1942, Elder George Brock served as pastor of Rough Creek for several years. It was told that the Spirit was so strong, when he was preaching, that sinners who came to stand outside and scoff or mock, were drawn by the Spirit to go inside to the altar to be saved. He had a strong church following during his 42 years of ministry. Many notable citizens of Laurel County were among his friends and congregation. Capt. John Brock and Levi Jackson were some of the first settlers in Laurel County. He arrived in 1802 and claimed a large tract of land along the Wilderness Road. The park in Laurel County is called Levi Jackson State Park. Elder George Brock had a long ministry during this time.

Most ministers did not receive money, as they do now. Back then, they had another way of supporting their families. Although most didn't have the same bills we have today. Most would grow their own food or raise livestock and owned their properties out right. Elder George Brock had a large family. They lived on a one-hundred-acre farm they purchased in 1841. It was mostly hilly, but for a few level fields. They raised grain and grew corn and wheat, which they took to the mill, to be ground into meal and flour.

He used oxen to help make his farm work somewhat easier, if you could say that about the work in those days. Back then, there was far more physical labor. They would pull the plows as he steered them. The men worked the fields, and the women usually took care of the vegetables and fruit orchards. They would harvest the vegetables and fruit and store canned and dried fruit for the winter months ahead. They raised hogs and chickens and cured the meat in the Smokehouse on their property. Their chickens supplied them with fresh eggs, and the cows they owned supplied them with fresh milk, as needed. They also churned their own butter. The Brock family had a stream called Rocky Brock. The stream ran to Little Laurel River, just a few hundred feet from their home. This became a popular place for people who were traveling. They would stop and refresh themselves with cool water and water their horses, or whatever animals they may be traveling with.

Elder George Brock was the pastor of Rough Creek United Baptist Church for 37 years. Brock, my fourth great-grandfather, passed away at the old homestead in 1879. He was buried in Rough Creek Cemetery, five miles from London, Kentucky.

George Brock's father, Banner Brock, my fifth great-grandfather, died in 1815 during service in the War of 1812. George was orphaned after his father's death and raised by his uncle, Capt. John Brock. Evidence states that George's mother never applied for a pension after his father's death, but Elder George Brock lived a great life and shared his testimony with all who met him. It is because of him I have such deep ties and deep roots in the Christian faith. I have a great heritage in my bloodline, and I am grateful for it.

My mother's father, Elmer Parker, was born in 1913. He didn't have any sons until four daughters were born to him and Dora, my mom's mother. She said they had some mules, and she loved those mules. They worked them in the fields to plow the hollers of Knox County. There were a lot of steep hills around that area with some flat places for planting. She worked with him in the fields, but said she didn't mind. They'd sell corn in Barboursville in the summer. In those days, most of the men were farmers, so they trapped furs and sold mink to make money. I remember vaguely that he had turkey shoots, where men would come and pay to get chances to shoot at a target. Whoever was the best won the turkey. Several men loved and enjoyed this.

My grandfather loved gospel and bluegrass music. He, my grandmother, and my aunts sang mostly gospel music. My mother can play just about any instrument she puts her hands on. She mostly plays an electric guitar. She even had a record made! Some with her mom and dad and siblings called Betty Williams and the Parker Family. No one has ever taught her, but she can play the banjo, mandolin, fiddle, harmonica, piano, and guitar. I got a little bit from her, I can play the piano, and I played with her in church for several years. She has always had a passion for music. She's played the guitar in church for over forty years. She is almost 76 and still plays in church, to this day.

I remember her sitting out on the porch playing the guitar when I was a kid. Need I remind you, it's electric—she was playing it to a large amp, as loud as she could! I was very shy and the thought of our neighbors hearing her play embarrassed me to death! Not that she couldn't play well, because she could play very well. I was just shy. We lived in the country, and there were only one or two close neighbors. My mom used to play her guitar a lot, even on days she wasn't in church. If it was nice outside, she'd be sitting on the front porch, probably playing something by Johnny Cash. She could play just like him—or better, I thought. When my siblings were young, before I came along, she would play it for four of them and tell them to dance, and they would do a little jig all over that porch! They'd dance and dance and have a ball dancing to her playing! She loved to tape record audio on those little recorders you could buy in those days. She loved to send some home to her mom and dad and siblings. I remember her saying, "Now be real quiet, because I'm going to tape some songs," and she would record herself singing and playing.

In the early to mid-80s, when it was just my brother Tony and I left in the house, she used to make me us come from playing in our rooms to watch the Rev. Billy Graham preach on TV. I kind of dreaded when he came on, because I knew I was going to have to sit there about an hour or longer. She would say, "Y'all better be quiet and not get up and make a noise." It's hard for little kids to do that, but we did. If anything, it instilled in me a love for God, and, when I was eight, I got saved in that little country church in Hillsboro, Kentucky. Since writing this, the famous Rev. Billy Graham passed away at 99 years of age, on February 21, 2018. He was quoted as saying, "Someday, you will read or hear that Billy Graham is dead. Don't you believe a word of it. I shall be more alive than I am now. I will just have changed my address. I will have gone into the presence of God."

My dad didn't go to church at all with my mom until I was around twelve, but when he did, he gave his heart to God. I can say my mom and dad have been very faithful in their walk with Christ and very faithful to the house of God. My mom, now 75, rarely misses a service and still plays her guitar in church. They have been examples of good character for me to look up to. I see my mom help people many people wouldn't help. A homeless-looking man named Scrammy, had dirty and torn clothes and smelled like something awful, but my mom would give him money or just help him out. I've seen her help so many people. Some, in my heart I thought, didn't need it, but she'd do it anyway. My dad was the same way. My mom told me of a time when she was young and could get a candy bar for five cents or a soda for five cents. She would milk the cows her parents owned, and she'd sell a gallon to her grandma Parker for 25 cents.

Her aunts, sisters, and father owned grocery stores in London. She would walk to the store Frank and Nile Craft owned one that was a half mile or less away. They were sisters who both owned grocery stores in the area. Neither one had any children. One day, she and her cousin, Elizabeth, whom she was very close to, had a boiled egg, bread, and jelly. She said in those days, they took their lunch, because there weren't always stores nearby. They decided to stop at Frank and Nile Craft's store. She said they took those eggs because they wanted some gum "real bad"—they didn't tell her they were boiled, though.

In those days, they candled the eggs. This method used embryology to study for growth and development of an embryo inside the eggs. With this method, you used a bright light source placed behind the eggs to show details through the shell. Since candles were the first source of light used, they called it candling. She said her aunt used a box and put a bright light to check the eggs brought in the store. They usually bought them from people who were selling them, but they would check to see if they were good or spoiled. Afterward, they would trade the eggs for the chewing gum. She checked their eggs after they left the store, only to find out they were boiled! She wasn't too happy, because she told her and Elizabeth's parents what they had done.

Her other aunt was Lizzie Gillian. She was the sister to Nile Craft. She owned a store just outside of Corbin. It was a large grocery store that sold everything. She also owned little cabins they rented out to people. My mother said this was sometime in the 1940s. Mom loved the mules that they owned. She said she and her sister Janice would often ride them for play. Mom said she would make sure to get the fastest mule. She often rode them bareback. Grandma Parker (my mom's grandmother, on her dad's side) lived half a mile away from them.

My mother's cousin Charly stayed with Grandma Parker. He had been in a house fire and, somehow, it caused him to become blind. One day, she decided she wanted to bring him to her house. Mind you, he didn't get out much in those days. It was just hard to lead a blind person. But she decided she would lead him to her place, which would have been a long trek for him with no sight, and her having to lead him all the way! So, she thought, "Oh no! What have I gotten myself into? This was a lot of work, and it was time-consuming leading him that far!" Then, of course, she had to do it all over again for him to get back home! She went to take him toys sometimes or things he could feel since he couldn't see them. He kept a box under his bed with the things she brought him to feel—he loved them! She liked to play games with him. Sometimes, when she walked into her grandmother's house, her grandmother would be busy in the other room, so she would sneak into Charly's room real quietly and shake his bed. She was about 12 when she picked on him like that. She said he was a real nice man, and she enjoyed visiting with him when she did. She hated that he had lost his vision from the fire.

Don't forget your childhood or your memories! Sometimes, when things are gone, that's all we have left—or maybe a picture. Times of fun, slower-paced living, times of the past and our history, times of communities coming together, working together, times of the old country stores on every corner, are gone but not forgotten. In my case, I'm one of the lucky ones who had gotten a chance to save an old general country store from our community: the Old Mayo General Store, now known as Vicky's Mayo Country Store and Café.

The house I was born in on Tatham Ridge Rd.

My siblings & me being the baby at the house I was born in 1976

Mt. Olivet Baptist Church in Tatham

First Mt. Olivet Baptist Church in Tatham 1800s

Old Iron Bridge. Across the Tatham River, you can see Mt. Olivet Baptist Church on the right of the bridge.

Tatham Springs, Washington County

Tathum Springs Hotel & Spa in Tatham

Picture of Tatham Springs Hotel & Spa swimming pool.

Tatham Springs Hotel & Spa in Thatham.

People getting baptized in the river under the iron bridge in Tatham

Henry Royalty's store I went to as a young child in Tatham.

The Road to My Old Kentucky Home

Brother Lowell Cantrell and his wife. He was pastor at Mt. Olivet. Baptist Church from 1973 to 1978.

Me as a child on Tatham Ridge in Willisburg Ky year 1976.

Mayo store in Mayo, Kentucky, in 1912. The owner, Van Carter, is last person on the right, and the person to his left is future owner A.R. Brown

A.R. Brown's store in Mayo in the 1970s.

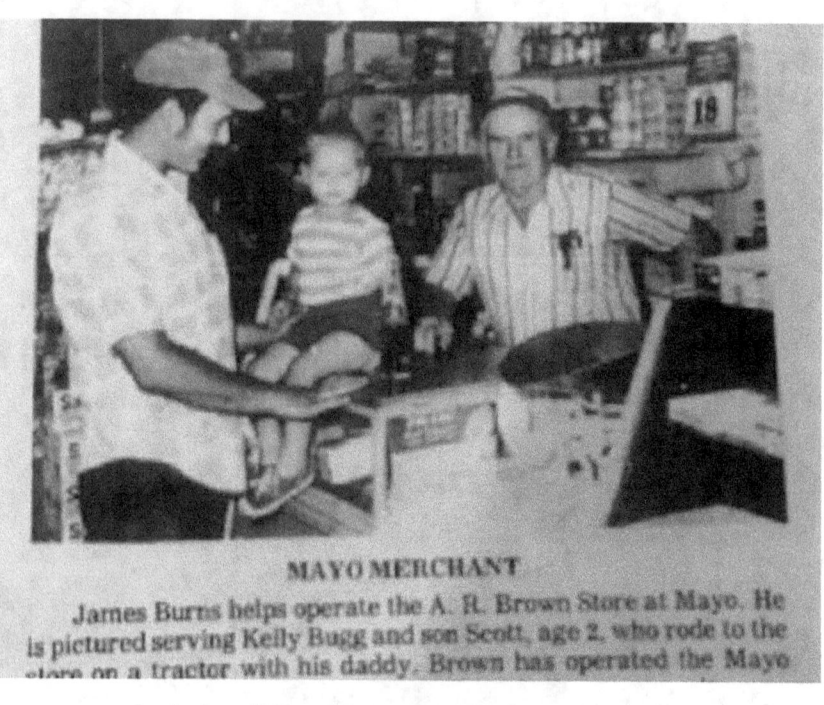

In the late 1970s, A.R. Brown still operates the store

A.R. Brown, the owner of the Mayo store for over 60 years.

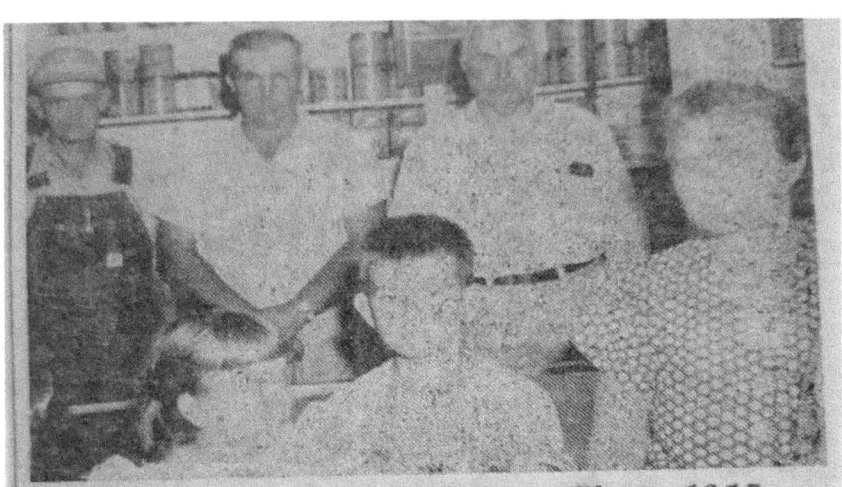

Brown Store in Mayo.

Picture of the Mayo Store I purchased, taken in 2018.

*A. R. Brown in his younger years.
Owner of Mayo General store for over 60 years.*

A. R. Brown sitting behind the long counter at Mayo store in the 1970s.

Pictures of inside the 100+ year-old store as we clean it.

The old original Skylight inside the Mayo store.

*Inside view of the old Mayo store.
We were working at the time of the picture.*

Old Hillsboro Church I attended as a young girl in Washington County. Where I got saved at when I was eight years old

Another view Of Hillsboro Church in Washington County, Kentucky.

Don Grays old store when I was growing up

RURAL STORE
Angela Goodlett, age 3, watches transaction at Goodlett's Grocery, Mayo, as her mother, Mrs. Carol Goodlett (at cash register) waits on customer Mrs. Bill Wilson. The two women's husbands operate a meat processing business at Mayo.

The top picture was taken in 2017, and the bottom picture was taken in the mid-1970s.

 # Meaux Chapel
Central Pike

Our seventh, and last, property is Meaux Chapel, located a short distance from the community of Mayo on Central Pike. Meaux Chapel is an African Methodist Episcopal church established sometime before 1870, almost certainly by the slaves John Meaux emancipated in his will of 1826 and confirmed by decree of the Mercer County Chancery court in 1837.

When some of the 60 (give or take several) slaves who found themselves free prior to the Civil War also became landowners in the Mayo area, that was the start of that community having a significant number of black families settled there and becoming farmers. As was the custom, the Meaux surname was taken by most of the John Meaux slaves, and to this day the Meaux name is spread far and wide throughout the county. This small African American church was originally a log structure, having massive logs cut from the virgin timber in the area.

Those logs are visible from the removal of part of the siding that later covered the building. Although there are no longer services held there, the building is still a part of the black community of Mayo, which also included the Mayo Colored School and the Dividing Ridge Baptist Church and cemetery.

Meaux Chapel is privately owned and we do not know how much longer he will extend his kindness toward it and allow it to be "discovered" by passers by. It is an important part of our Mercer County African American history with a very uncertain future.

Old Fairview school on ll60 talmage Mayo Rd Mercer ky

1930s, when it started operating as a school.

The Road to My Old Kentucky Home

On Central Pike Rd Harrodsburg Ky
Juncture of Eldorado-Dugansville Turnpike
And Central Turnpike

This was Con Johnson's house , I think Wendell Johnson lived here too if I recollect ,
This was the Toll-Gatehouse that sat in front of Mayo Christian Church

Fee if walking 05 cents
But by Horse or Buggy 10 cents

The first Mayo General Store in 1885,
located on same property as the 1912 one.

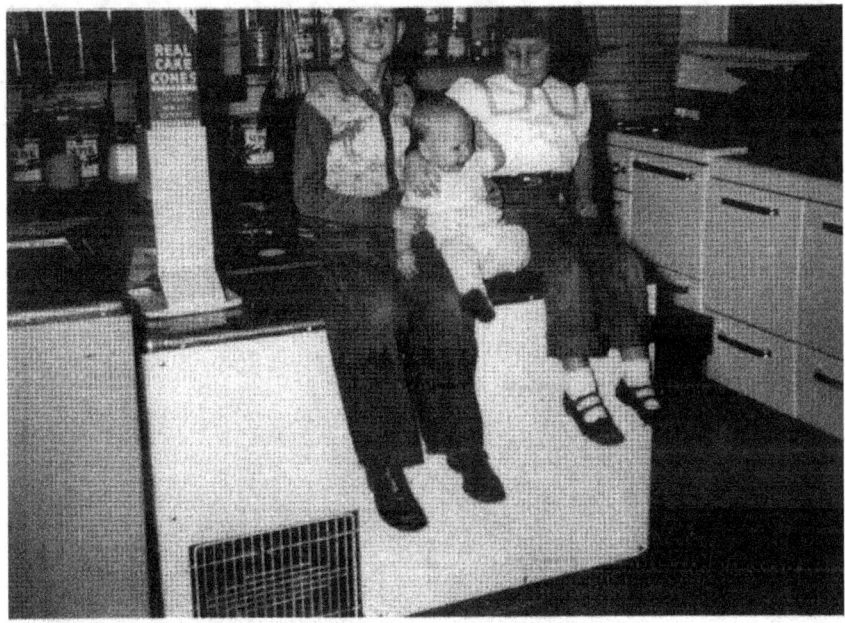

A.R. Brown's store in Mayo, Kentucky,
with his grandchildren in the store.

The land between tracts #2 and #4 is our property.

Tablow Store near Bethel Baptist Church in Mercer County, Kentucky.

Dugansville store at 1160 Talmage Mayo Road in the early 1900s.

Duncan Store in Mercer County, Kentucky in the early 1900s.

Duncan Store 1900 in Mercer County, Kentucky.

Twin Hill Drive-In in Harrodsburg, Kentucky.

Mooresville Bridge in Springfield, Kentucky.

Mooresville Bridge on a snowy day in January 2018.

Mooresville Covered Bridge.

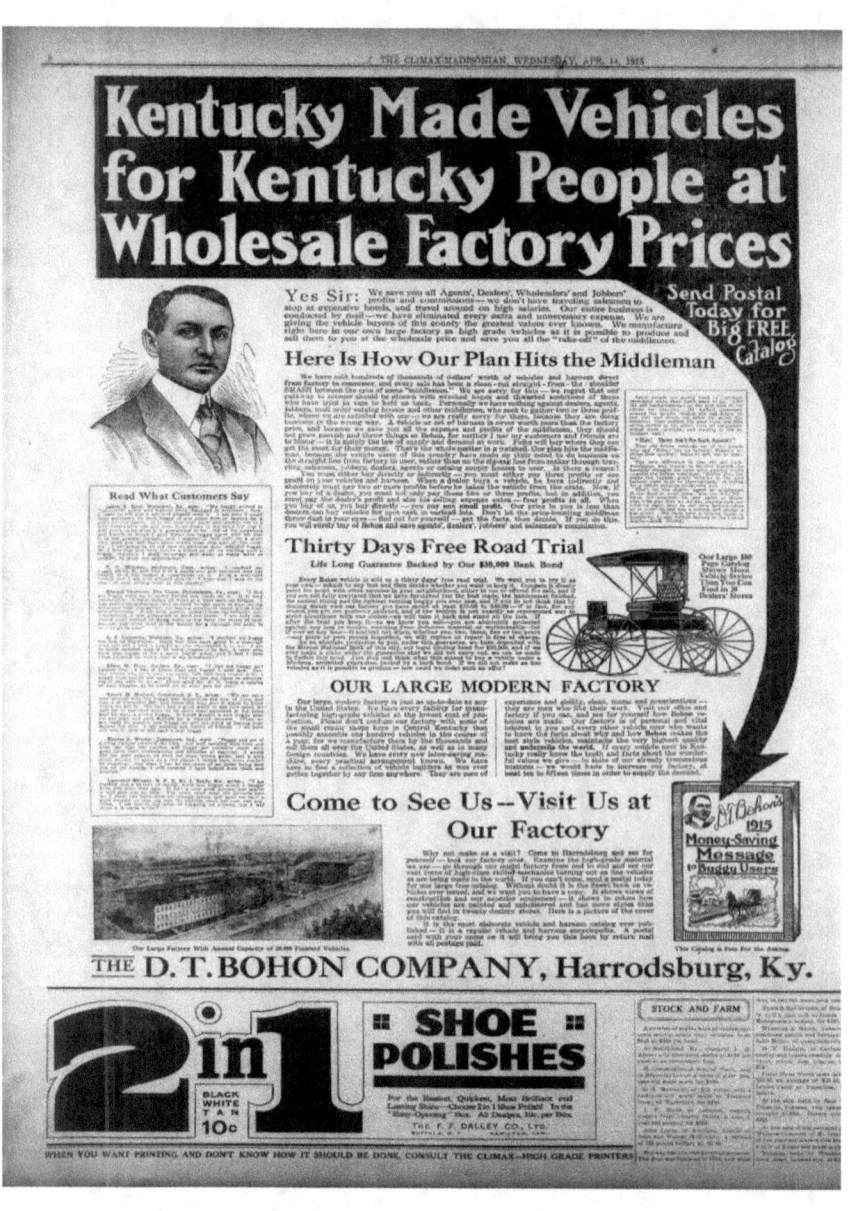

Bohon's Buggie company ad.

Bohon Buggy Company in Harrodsburg, Kentucky.

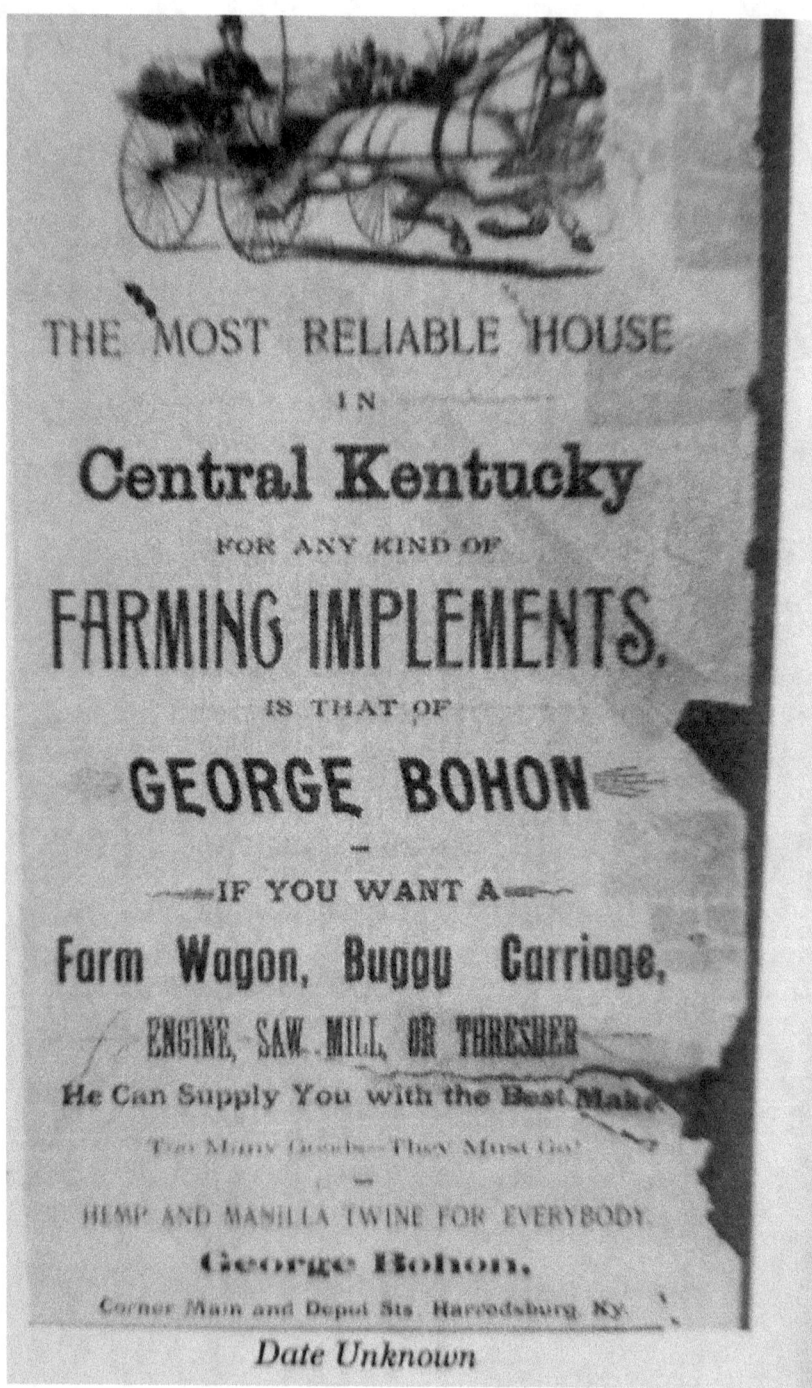

Bohon Buggy ad from the late 1800s or early 1900s.

Bohon Buggy Company in Harrodsburg, Kentucky in the 1920s.

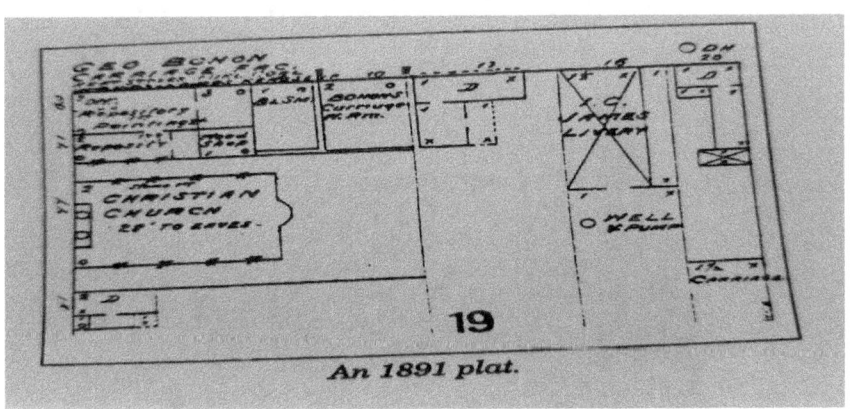

The Road to My Old Kentucky Home

George Bohon's Buggy before 1900.

Carriers Store. Willisburg, Kentucky.

Hopewell Baptist Church, which served a school for the children of Mayo in the early 1900s.

Cane Ridge meeting house.

*Shaker Village, Harrodsburg, Kentucky.
The spiral staircase was built by Micajah.*

Burnett at age 17 in the 1800s.

Graham Springs Resort and Spa in Harrodsburg, Kentucky.

The Graham Springs Resort and Spa, known for its curing waters.

Graham Springs Hotel book ticket in the famous spa days of early 1800s to early 1900s.

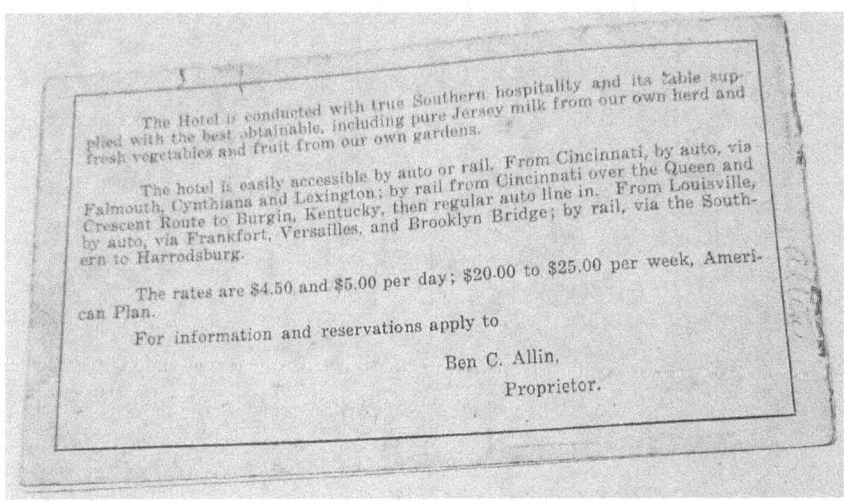

Rates at the Graham Springs Hotel and Spa.

Christopher Columbus Graham

*Old historic Mayo General store,
now owned by me as Vickie's Mayo Country Store.*

www.ingramcontent.com/pod-product-compliance
Lightning Source LLC
LaVergne TN
LVHW020427080526
838202LV00055B/5065